Copyright © 2019 by Riley M

All rights reserved. No part of this publication may be reproduced, distributed, or transmitted in any form or by any means, including photocopying, recording, or other electronic or mechanical methods, without the prior written permission of the publisher, except in the case of brief quotations embodied in critical reviews and certain other noncommercial uses permitted by copyright law

Table of Contents

WHAT IS AN AMAZON FBA BUSINESS? 5
    HOW TO SOURCE YOUR PRODUCTS 7
    HOW TO DO MARKET RESEARCH ON AMAZON 9
GETTING YOUR STOCK FROM ALIBABA TO AMAZON FBA 10
    Pricing 11
    Finding A Manufacturer 14
    Prototyping 15
    Negotiation and Manufacturing 16
    Freight Forwarding & Customs 18
AMAZON AND AMAZON FBA 18
    Creating the Listing on Amazon 19
    Sending Stock to Amazon FBA 21
    Marketing 23
HOW TO GET REVIEWS ON AMAZON 26
    EXPAND TO DIFFERENT COUNTRIES 31
    EXPAND TO DIFFERENT PRODUCTS 31
TIPS AND TRICKS FOR MARKETING YOUR AMAZON FBA BUSINESS 32
    GETTING MORE VIEWS ON YOUR LISTINGS FROM AMAZON 34
    Pay-Per-Click Advertising On Amazon 35

Setting Up An Automatic Campaign 36

Setting Up A Manual Campaign 39

Amazon Search Optimisation 40

GETTING VIEWS ON YOUR LISTING FROM OUTSIDE AMAZON
.... 43

Giveaways & Deals On Offer Sites 45

Pay-Per-Click Advertising 46

IMPROVING THE CONVERSIONS OF YOUR LISTINGS 47

Good Description 50

Getting Good Reviews 50

PROS & CONS OF THE THREE TYPES OF AMAZON FBA BUSINESS
.... 56

Retail Arbitrage 56

Private Labelling 59

Brand Building 63

EVERY TOOL I USE FOR MY AMAZON SELLER BUSINESS 66

Market Research 66

Sourcing Your Product 67

Cheap Foreign Currency Payments 67

Import, Logistics and Customs Clearance 68

Warehousing & Fulfilment 69

Marketing 69

Bookkeeping And Accountancy 71

HOW FULFILLMENT BY AMAZON (FBA) WORKS 72

    SELLING YOUR PRODUCTS ON AMAZON: A BRAND'S GUIDE 73

    STOCK UP 74

    REVIEWS RULE 74

    THE BUY BOX 76

    WHAT PRICE IS RIGHT 76

    ADVERTISING OPTIONS 77

WHAT IS AN AMAZON FBA BUSINESS?

I am sure you have heard of Amazon. It is the largest online retailer in the USA, UK and much of Europe. A household name. But what you might not know is that when you purchase something from Amazon, there is a very good chance that you are buying from a third party seller using a service called Amazon FBA.

FBA stands for 'fulfilment by Amazon'. What is means is that Amazon looks after all of the seller's stock. When a customer places an order, it by-passes the seller altogether and goes straight to the FBA warehouse. Amazon then picks out the order and delivers it to the customer.

Amazon FBA also handles most of the customer service. They process all customer returns and only the most specific queries get forwarded on to the seller. To the customer, there is almost no difference between purchasing from Amazon directly and from a person selling their items on Amazon through Amazon FBA. They get the same delivery options, the same returns policy and the same customer service team.

An Amazon FBA business is a great intermediary between a bedroom eBay business, and a full-time brand with a large staff. As a seller, you don't have to look after the stock and it takes the same amount of work to sell 10,000 items as it does to sell 10. But to the customer, they get a quality of service that is on par with the biggest brands in the word.

As a seller, you can run a one-man-band business that sells thousands of items each month, all remotely from anywhere in the world. In fact, I am currently in South America with Amazon FBA businesses in Europe and North America.

You acquire the stock and get it delivered to Amazon FBA. Then all you need to do is focus on getting sales.

In this chapther, we will talk about the main two types of Amazon FBA businesses. (there is one other type is completely different that I covered in this article: Retail Arbitrage).

Invent a product from scratch. Get it professionally designed and manufactured. Then work your arse off to try and convince people that they really want it and will buy it. This is the approach we follow and I documented for the table tennis bat cases in this book. It's a lot of work and you run the very real risk of discovering that people don't really want whatever you have invented.

Reinvent/improve on someone else's product. Simply find a not very good item that is selling well and create a better version of it. There are hundreds of items on Amazon that are just rebrands of readily available white-label products. You can even find the same factory that makes the original item and get them to do your manufacturing. As of 2016, this is the easiest and still a very profitable route to take.

HOW TO SOURCE YOUR PRODUCTS

We've spoken a lot about Amazon, but there is another global company that is almost as important. Alibaba.

Alibaba is a Chinese online wholesale market where factories and distributors from all around the world display their items. Most of these companies will work with you to create and manufacture your unique product.

Since Alibaba came on the scene it has got very easy to create a basic Amazon FBA business. Too easy. And has led to Amazon getting flooded with white-labelled products that are straight from Alibaba with a brand attached and a huge price markup. Most of them don't sell well, but there are plenty that do.

Here's an example. The only difference between the two is the adding of a brand name... and the price increase.

You can buy them in bulk on Alibaba, branded with your own brand for between $1 and $7 each (depending on how many you purchase and how good you are at negotiating), and people are buying them on Amazon for £16.95. Even with all the fees and costs (which we will talk about later), that is still a very good profit margin.

Now I can't be 100% sure that it is the same factory that makes both of them. But it doesn't really matter. Provided the factory is able to make us a better version, then we're in business.

Now that pest repeller looks pretty low quality, but you can also find very high quality, well-respected brands on Alibaba.

On the Alibaba factories' website, they describe themselves as: "the official supplier of 'RDX' one of the world's leading fitness brand, along with many other brands.".

I am not suggesting that you should try and create fake RDX gloves. That would be unethical and also bad business – it wouldn't take long before you were shut down. But I am suggesting that if you can come up with an improvement to the boxing glove, you could legitimately contact that factory on Alibaba, get your own unique boxing gloves made, add your own branding and start competing with RDX. Getting a really good idea for a product can take quite a bit of time and research, and is worth not rushing. In fact it is a full topic in its own right.

HOW TO DO MARKET RESEARCH ON AMAZON

To get an idea of what is selling and for how much I use a market research tool called Jungle Scout. It is a deep search tool for Amazon that compares each listing with its own data to work out how much your competitors are selling a month. It costs $69 a month (for the web app version with niche-hunter I am using below) and you can cancel it once you've chosen a product.

I am currently in the process of starting a new Amazon FBA business selling gin (Warning: I don't recommend you start with something as complex as alcohol), here are some real screenshots I took from my own market research in October 2017:

You can see that it includes a lot of the information that would be useful for finding a product that is selling well with not great reviews. And here is the niche hunter for going deeper and looking for keywords. It seems that there is a gap in the market selling strawberry gin:

There is more to finding a good product (size, weight and price is also important), but we don't need to go into that much detail right now. If you're interested you can bookmark this post and come back to it later.

GETTING YOUR STOCK FROM ALIBABA TO AMAZON FBA

The final piece of the puzzle to setting up an Amazon FBA business is how you get your stock in bulk from the factory to the FBA warehouses. On the surface, it can be very complicated. Every country has different customs processes and Amazon have some pretty complex requirements for how they need your items to be delivered.

Thankfully there are plenty of companies that deal with all the hassle for you and make it really easy, they are known as freight forwarders and customs brokers. I recommend Flexport. They are funded by Google, have a really good online interface and due to the transparent price comparison service, are cheap.

The steps are fairly simple:

The factory delivers the stock to the Flexport freight forwarder.

The freight forwarder gets the stock into your destination country and deals with all taxes and paperwork. The freight forwarder hands the stock over to the Amazon partnered couriers who books them into the FBA warehouses.

Simple eh? Well that's the basics of an Amazon FBA business:

- Find a factory on Alibaba.
- Open conversations with them and design your product.
- Get a large batch of the item manufactured.
- Use a freight forwarder such as Flexport to get the items from the factory to Amazon.
- Get marketing and sell your items.

Now let's dive into the nitty gritty.

Pricing

If you have done some browsing on Alibaba, you may be a bit shocked at how cheap the factories are selling wholesale quantities of their goods for. Unfortunately, it's not quite as simple as taking the price you sell it for and minusing the price you paid, There are a lot of costs to include.

I am talking about pricing and margin early on because it is so important. You can't start talking to manufacturers until you know how much margin you need.

Luckily Amazon has a handy calculator that you can use for most of the costs:

Just find an item similar to yours, or enter in your product's dimensions.

On top of these costs, there are a few other ones you need to add in manually.

The price of the item.

Shipping to the country.

Tax and customs charges.

Delivery to the Amazon FBA warehouses.

You can talk to Flexport and the Alibaba factories to get all these costs.

A typical example might be:

You expect to be able to sell the item for $16

It costs $4 per item to buy.

Shipping is $1 per item.

Tax and import duties are $0.75 per item.

Delivery to the FBA warehouse is $0.2 per item.

FBA fulfilment fees are $3.05 per item.

Amazon closing fee is 15% of sale price, so $2.4.

Your profit is $4.6 per item.

That is still a good margin and provided we can get sales is a good Amazon FBA business.

Because of the way the Amazon fees work, your ideal product will be:

Selling for between £15 and £50 ($20 and $70).

Small and lightweight.

Simple and with not too many moving parts.

And of course, an item that people want to buy. As mentioned earlier, finding the best products to sell on Amazon has it's own whole post here. In short, there are a few great tools that can help you research the ideal product. JungleScout is probably the best and most popular.

Once you understand how the margin and fees work, the next step is to start chatting with some manufacturers.

Finding A Manufacturer

I suggest talking with as many factories as possible. With Alibaba it is so easy, just use the search bar for whatever you are looking for and click "contact supplier" next to the companies that look interesting.

When searching add the word 'OEM' to the end of your search. For instance "Flashlight OEM". It stands for 'original object manufacture' and should filter out all the re-sellers and give you the factories that actually manufacture the items.

You might as well shoot off the same message to lots of different factories and then play them off against each other. The factories know the value of even a new Amazon FBA business and will want to work with you.

It is very hard to describe what I look for in a good factory beyond "a good feeling". I think it comes with practice. I suggest that once you have spoken to them, try having a chat over Skype. If their English is so bad you can't really communicate, then it is probably not going to work out.

Once you have narrowed down your search to your favourite 3 or 4 factories, ask them to send you out a sample. Some places will send you one for free, others will charge you but then take the cost off any large order you eventually make. A few will ask you to pay full price. Once you have samples from a couple of factories you are happy with, it is time to move onto the next step.

Prototyping

Now remember, we are not just looking to re-sell their products. We want to improve and customise them.

This process can take quite a long time, but it is worth getting right. If you can get the designs done professionally, that could really help to really speed the process up. You can hire a freelancer on Freelancer to help you.

Or you can make amateur suggestions and ask the factory to turn them into products. Here are some designs we made in Microsoft Paint for our table tennis bat cases. One of the keys to an Amazon FBA business is keeping costs as low as possible. So make sure to think through what is the best use of your money.

During this design phase, you need to incorporate a barcode. A barcode (or UPC code) is a series of digits that is unique to your product all over the world. There are plenty of websites where you can buy barcodes, this is the website I use. Once you have the perfect prototype it is time to get them manufactured.

Negotiation and Manufacturing

Although I hate negotiating, on Alibaba it is a requirement. You can often get 40%-70% off the asking price.

As it is so easy for customers to price compare a lot of factories are starting to realise that they can get more business by opening with their best price. But I think it will still be another few years before you don't need to negotiate.

You may be great at haggling and love competing for the best price. If on the other handyou're more like my, here are my thirty seconds on negotiating on Alibaba.

There are a few things we really care about:

- Minimum Order Requirement.
- Price.
- Lead Time.

At the beginning, the first one is the most important. You may be able to get a great deal if you order 10,000 items, but that would be crazy for a new product you haven't tried to sell yet. If no-one buys it you're left paying storage on 10,000 items! I recommend starting with about 500.

On lead time, sometimes the factories can take months to create your product. If you're just starting out you may well be willing to sacrifice a bit of margin to get your products to Amazon quicker.

If you have a few different good options for manufacturer you can play them off against each other on choose the best deal.

The only other thing I would say about negotiating is: don't burn your bridges. The first manufacturer may turn out to be a dud and you may want that second one. So even if you don't go with them, leave the option open for future business.

When you finally give them the go-ahead, make sure to request that the items are packaged together in the same size cartons. This will be important when organising the final part of the delivery to Amazon.

Freight Forwarding & Customs

I've already mentioned that Flexport or another freight forwarder will do most of the work of shipping and customs for you. They're generally good enough that I don't need to go into much more detail. Except to talk about shipping options.

You have the choice of sending your stock by ship or by plane. A shipment from China to the UK or the USA will take 6-8 weeks. By plane, it will take less than a week. But plane will be about five times more expensive.

If I am running low I will fly in some emergency stock, but the majority I send by boat. On your initial order you could always send a small amount, say 60, by plane and the rest by boat. That way you can be up and selling much quicker.

AMAZON AND AMAZON FBA

Once your shipment has landed in the destination country you need to get it to the Amazon warehouses. But first, you will need to create an Amazon account. I strongly suggest creating the account before you start manufacturing.

It is free to sign-up as an 'Individual' Amazon seller in most countries and anyone from most countries can do it. India is the only exception that I know of, there you need to have an India-based business to register. I suggest starting with just one country, the one you are most local to:

Amazon UK (includes Germany, Italy, France & Italy).

Amazon USA (includes Mexico & Canada).

Amazon India (you need to have an Indian based business to sign up)

There are two types of Amazon accounts. Individual and Professional.

Individual is free but you pay an extra fee per item sold, you also have access to less analytics.

Professional charges a monthly fee.

Both can be used with Amazon FBA, so I simply suggest signing up for an individual account and upgrading once your sales hit the threshold where the professional account is cheaper.

Creating the Listing on Amazon

Once you have finished creating your account. From the homepage navigate to the inventory tab and select "Add a Product". Select "Create a new product listing". Then select the most relevant category.

You will then be taken to the details page of your new product. There are hundreds of fields, but most of them you can safely ignore as they don't really add anything. Make sure to fill out:

Under 'Vital Info'

Item Name. I like to include the brand name here as well as it it is what the customer sees when searching through Amazon. e.g. "Awesomo Fly Swatter Mk2"

Brand Name. This is your Amazon FBA business brand. e.g. "Awesomo"

Recommended Browse Node.

Product ID. This is the UPC number that you purchased when designing the product. It is the unique barcode.

Under 'Offer'

Your Price.

Condition.

Fulfilment Channel = 'I want Amazon to dispatch and provide customer service for my items if they sell.'

The fulfilment channel is important. This is where you tell Amazon that you want to create an Amazon FBA business and have Amazon handle your stock and customer service for you.

Under 'Images'

Images are very important. Make sure you have someone take some professional looking photographs of your item.

Under 'Description'

Make full use of this page and make your product sound as appealing as possible.

Keywords

Enter a few alternative words that people might search for your item. For instance, if you are selling a pest repeller they might also search for 'bug repeller' or 'mosquito repeller'.

And that's all you need. Now click 'Save and Finish'.

Sending Stock to Amazon FBA

Provided you selected that you want Amazon to fulfil your items, you will next be sent to the 'Send/Replenish Inventory' page.

Just follow the instructions. At some point, you will be asked for some more details about your item, including the proportions and weight. Every product sent to Amazon needs to be labelled with a label that is unique for the item and shipment ID. This is an internal barcode that Amazon uses to track and manage inventory. You can either get your freight forwarder to do this or pay Amazon to do it.

I've found that the freight forwarder is normally a cheaper option, but there's not much in it and it is more work on your behalf. To get them to do it you need to negotiate it as an added extra, then download and send them the PDFs of the labels. Once you have clicked through all the steps you will have a chance to review and accept the shipment. Once it is created select 'Work on Shipment' to tell Amazon how it is going to be delivered. The easiest way is to select 'Small Parcel Delivery' and choose the 'Amazon Partnered Carrier'.

Remember how we made sure that all the cartons sent by the factory were of the same size and weight? This is why.

By using the 'Amazon Partnered Carrier' (which is UPS) you will pre-pay for delivery based on the number and proportions of the boxes you are sending. Amazon will then generate you a pre-paid label in the form of a PDF file. Just gives these PDF files to the freight forwarder, they will attach them to the cartons and give them to UPS. Next thing you know your stock will be at Amazon.

And that's it... once your stock arrives your Amazon FBA business will be live and people will be able to buy and receive the items without you even having to be told about it. Well not quite. If you just leave it, no-one will buy your product. The final step in the puzzle is also the most difficult. How on earth do you get people to buy your items?

Marketing

In my experience, I have found the best way to get decent sales for a new product on a new Amazon FBA business is to do a short sharp burst and try get as high up as possible on the best-seller rankings. Once there the Amazon algorithm will start showing the item to people searching on the website.

Let me explain.

When you start a new Amazon FBA business. You have zero reviews and zero sales. You don't even have an Amazon seller ranking. There is no reason for the customer or Amazon to trust your product is any good.

Amazon has a secret formula that determines what shows up when people search for something. It's secret but we can take a guess at how logically it could work. It is known as the Amazon Search algorithm.

Let's pretend that I am the Amazon algorithm, and it's my job to choose what we show people who are using the site. Imagine someone searches for a teapot. How do I choose from the hundreds of teapots which ones to show the user?

Well, I think my first instinct would be just to rank all the teapots on Amazon by how well they're selling. Put the best-selling one at the top and the worst selling one at the bottom.

But that's a bit too simple. What happens if the best selling teapot is just a big brand name that is rubbish but they are spending a lot on advertising? People are still buying it but they are giving it bad reviews.

Ok, so ratings are important too, let's take that into account. Perhaps I show a better-reviewed teapot higher than a teapot that has slightly more sales.

But that's also too simple. What about a teapot that only has one review. Even if it's a 5-star review I can't show that higher than a teapot with 100 4.9 reviews. Ok, so I weight the rating in some way by the number of reviews.

But what if there is some new teapot technology out and the best-selling teapot is behind the times? It still has all those good reviews. And it is still the best-seller. But it is unfair because it has been around so long that it would take a new better teapot years to get the same number of reviews.

Ok now I am going to take into account momentum. An item that has only been around a few weeks but is getting a lot of sales and good reviews I will show in a high place.

Ahh. Now we're getting somewhere. We have no idea how exactly the algorithm balances these factors, but we can be pretty sure that it favours:

Sales, good reviews, many reviews, and momentum.

A brand new Amazon FBA business with no reviews and sales is not going to be shown to anyone. A brand new product that has a lot of sales in the first week and a lot of good reviews is going to be shown to people.

It is our job as a new seller to get as many new sales and reviews as possible in a short space of time. We need that momentum to start showing up organically on people's Amazon searches.

The simplest ways to do this is by:

1. Asking all your friends and family to buy and review your product.
2. Hosting a competition/giveaway.
3. Send free samples to professional & amateur reviewers.
4. Paid for advertising.
5. Asking previous customers to review your products.

HOW TO GET REVIEWS ON AMAZON

I have added this part in to expand on that final bullet point as it is what I get emailed about most. The best long term way to getting reviews is to convince your real customers to write them. Amazon is very strict on how you can interact with your customers but one thing you are allowed to do is to email them asking for a review. But they don't make it easy, there is no way to set up automated mass emails from inside Amazon Seller Central. Instead we have to use an outside service.

I personally use Feedback Genius. It is very simple to use and has a lot of customizability. There are different plans to choose from but the smallest one is free which allows up to 100 emails a month. Then $20 for the next 1,000 emails.

There are a lot of rules about what you can include in your emails. You cannot:

Incentivise a customer to leave a good review. That means no "get 20% off your next order if you leave a good review".

You cannot include a decision tree to filter different types of reviews. That means you are not allowed to say "if you loved the product click here to leave a good review, or if you were in any way unsatisfied please click here to message me directly and I will do everything I can to fix it".

You are also not allowed to include a link to your own website in the email.

You may not get caught if you break these rules. But if you are serious about your Amazon FBA business I strongly recommend you follow them. Amazon has been known to ban people from selling on their platform for inappropriate emailing. If that happens that is the end of your Amazon FBA business.

So if you can't include any of that, what can you include to encourage them to leave a good review? My personal preference is a two email chain.

The first email simply includes useful information about their purchase and asks that if they are unhappy to email me. Here is my template for some table tennis bats I sell, I change the wording slightly depending on the product and the audience:

Hi [[first-name]],

My name is Sam and I'm one of the creators of the xxxx. Thank you so much for your order!

I wanted to reassure you that we've got you covered. If you aren't completely satisfied with something when your order arrives, then let me know and we'll get it straightened out for you ASAP. Additionally, if you have any questions about your order or our products we'd be happy to help you out.

If you'd like to get in touch, you can just reply to this message and we'll respond promptly. No question is ever too small or unimportant. I'm going to provide some usage tips for your xxxx:

After receiving your bat, the first step is to remove the protective film on each of the black and red rubbers. The rubbers should feel a bit sticky to the touch. It's this surface that enables you to create the incredible spin that our bats are known for.

The bat should be stored in its case between use. If left out for a prolonged period of time the rubbers should be cleaned. As you use the bat, the rubbers will start to attract dust from the ball and will lose their feeling of stickiness. They can be cleaned by wiping them down with a bit of water on a clean cloth.

After about a year of heavy usage, the rubbers will slowly lose their spin and should be replaced. They are designed to be easily removed and new rubbers can be stuck down in their place. Alternatively, a new bat can be purchased. The bat has been tested and approved by the International Table Tennis Federation, meaning its legal for use at tournaments of any level. So go, win some matches and enjoy the bat!

All the best,

Sam

This email sets the tone for the level of customer service I want my Amazon FBA business to offer as well as heading off bad reviews before they happen.

My second email asks for a review:

Hey [[first-name]],

First off, I wanted to say thank you once again for your support. Our small business wouldn't be able to grow and continue to produce top quality table tennis bats without your help.

I noticed your order was delivered a couple days ago, so I hope that you've had the chance to try it out and make sure you are happy with everything.

We are always aiming to improve our products and service, and we would really appreciate if you could take 2 seconds to provide us with some feedback:

[[product-review-link:Leave a review]]

Thank you again for your trust and support.

As always, if you have any questions, suggestions or comments, or even just want to have a chat, send us a message by replying to this email and we'll get back to you as soon as possible.

All the best,

Sam

The text in square brackets is shortcode which Feedback Genius converts into links that are customised for each customer.

Once you have the marketing for your Amazon FBA business down and have conquered your own country, it's time to expand:

EXPAND TO DIFFERENT COUNTRIES

Once you have started to rank in one country it's time to expand and do the same in others.

The great thing is that with the central accounts of the UK and USA you can expand your selling to a bunch of other countries with just a few clicks.

For instance, with Amazon UK you can cross-list your items on Amazon Germany. When a customer buys your item in Germany it will be shipped to them from the UK FBA warehouse. Amazon even provides a translation service so that your listings will be spelt correctly in the target language. Congratulations! You now have a multi-national global Amazon FBA business.

EXPAND TO DIFFERENT PRODUCTS

Now you are selling strongly everywhere. Time to move on to a new product and start the whole process again. Except this time it should go much smoother and easier.

RECAP

Ok. So that was long and complicated. Let's quickly recap the steps to setting up an Amazon FBA business:

- Decide on a product idea.
- Find and open communication with relevant factories on Alibaba that manufacture similar items.
- Request samples and then commission prototypes to be made.
- Purchase a barcode.
- Start manufacturing.
- Use a freight forwarder such as Flexport to get your stock to the target country and through customs.
- Open an Amazon Seller Account and create your listings.
- Create a shipment on Amazon FBA and pre-pay for shipping.
- Give your freight forwarder the pre-paid shipping labels.
- Start marketing.

TIPS AND TRICKS FOR MARKETING YOUR AMAZON FBA BUSINESS

I have been selling on Amazon since 2013 and it has been my largest source of income since 2014. I love the business model and think that using Amazon FBA is the best way to build a scalable physical product brand in 2017. But I am seeing a disturbing trend. There are lots of people who have bought into the dream, invested a lot of money in creating a product and a first batch made, but haven't put any thought into how to sell it once it arrives in the Amazon warehouses. I hope to rectify that mistake in this chapther by telling you everything I know about marketing your Amazon FBA business.

This book is really for people who have set up or are in the process of setting up an Amazon FBA business.

Marketing your Amazon FBA business is first and foremost a creative endeavor – the marketing that works is the marketing that everyone else isn't doing. So let me put it bold:this is not a how-to guide, this is just a collection of tips and tricks that work for me. I suggest trying them all out and going with what works. In the words of Bruce Lee:

Absorb what is useful, discard what is useless and add what is specifically your own.

Now on to the goodies. There is a lot here so I am going to split my guide on marketing your Amazon FBA business into a few categories:

Getting More Views On Your Listings From Amazon

Including pay-per-click and Amazon search optimization

Getting Views On Your Listing From Outside Amazon

Including influencer marketing, giveaways, and traditional advertising

Improving the Conversions of Your Listings

Including listing improvement and getting more good reviews

GETTING MORE VIEWS ON YOUR LISTINGS FROM AMAZON

Appearing In Amazon Searches

The best way to get views on your Amazon listing is to appear at the top of the list when someone searches for the product. There are two ways to do this. Either: Get selected by Amazon's algorithm as the most relevant result for the searched for keyword.

Pay to be at the top.

In the below image I have done a quick search for 'water bottle' and put a red square around all the listings that have paid to be there and a green square around the organic ones. It is pretty bad really. If someone searches for 'water bottle' they need to scroll down before they get to any listings that haven't paid to be at the top.

Marketing your Amazon FBA business is quickly turning into a pay-to-play setup.

Pay-Per-Click Advertising On Amazon

Amazon PPC is pretty easy to understand and is the simplest way of marketing your Amazon FBA products. It is an auction based system. For each keyword everyone bids on how much they are willing to pay per click. Then Amazon chooses a winner based on the bid amount and how suitable they think your product is.

We don't know exactly how the auction works as it is secret. What we do know is that you don't pay the full bid amount. My best guess is that the winner pays the bid of the closest loser. So if I bid £10 a click and the next closest bid is 50p. I will pay 50p. That is a guess, but an educated one. It does make it quite difficult to choose a bidding strategy, luckily we can let Amazon do that for us. More on this later.

The system is the same regardless of which Amazon marketplace you are selling on. The below screenshot is from my Canadian seller account.

ACoS is one of the key figures. Provided this is better than your profit margin you will be making money. So if your profit margin is normally 40% after production costs and all Amazon fees, you will be making money for any ACoS below 40%. (If you're not a natural mathematician and are struggling to work out your profit margin you can use a third party Amazon seller analytics software, such as Fetcher).

Recently there has been a lot of complaints about Amazon PPC. In the USA it has got very competitive and the average ACoS people are seeing has been growing. Which is one of the reasons I have shown you my Canadian campaign manager in the screenshot above. My ACoS on every other marketplace is about half of what it is in the USA. Here is the exact same campaign on the USA site:

The ACoS is over double. In fact, it is so high that we almost make no money anymore. Marketing your Amazon FBA business on the USA site is getting very competitive, but that doesn't mean it isn't worth doing. I will run the PPC campaign even if it breaks even. Extra sales lead to more reviews (see below) and help you climb the bestseller rankings. So even if sales from the PPC campaign don't make any money, they should lead to more organic sales. (That's the theory anyway!)

Setting Up An Automatic Campaign

The most simple type of Amazon FBA PPC campaign is an automated one. Set a small daily budget (maybe $10 to begin with), choose the products you want to advertise, let Amazon choose your bid and then let it loose. It is that simple and takes just a few clicks.

Generally, I suggest doing a separate campaign for each item that is completely different and targeting different keywords. If you have items that target the same keyword, put them in the same campaign and the same ad group. If you put them in separate campaigns you risk bidding against yourself for the same keyword.

Amazon will automatically select keywords and bid on them for you.

After a week or two, you can go in and optimise the campaign by reviewing what it has been bidding on and telling it the keywords not to bid on. In the campaign manager click on 'download the search terms report' and open it in excel. Here is a screenshot of one of my search term reports:

Note: The combination of letters and numbers are ASINs of other product. That means that my product appears as a suggested alternative to other seller's products.

I am looking for any search terms that are out of place and shouldn't be there. It seems that Amazon is struggling to tell the difference between the search term 'table tennis racket' and 'tennis racket'. I therefore need to go in and tell Amazon not to bid on 'tennis racket'.

If you're a bit of stats geek you can also look into which exact keywords or competitor products aren't converting and remove them too. There is a lot of good data in those search term reports!

Back in campaign manager we go to 'Campaign Settings' -> 'Negative Keywords'

The only thing to be aware of here is the difference between Phrase and Exact. Phrase includes any search term that has your keywords in that order in it. It also allows for variation of punctuation and capitals.

So in this example, phrase would also include:

Best mens tennis racket

mens tennis racket gift ideas

the very best men's tennis racket for father's day

Exact requires that the keywords to be the only words in the search term. But does allow for different punctuation and capitals. Exact would include:

This is important. For 'mens tennis racket' I am happy to add it as a negative phrase. But for the term 'tennis racket' I only want to add that as a negative exact. If I added it as a phrase I would also be telling Amazon to not bid on keywords such as 'table tennis racket', which is the opposite of what I'm trying to achieve!

And that is all I am going to say about automatic keyword targeting. Just log in periodically, make sure it is still profitable and tweak. Once the campaign has a profitable ACoS you can start raising the daily limit until you are spending all the Amazon will allow.

Setting Up A Manual Campaign

If you want to take a more hands on approach you can choose to set the keywords yourself. Some people have a lot of success doing this, but in my opinion it is only worth doing in a few very specific situations: where you have a high converting exact phrase you want to bid on. If you have a profitable exact phrase then it is worth it because your bid can be slightly lower.

In this image, I am creating a campaign targeting the keyword 'Water Bottle'. There are three levels of matching. Exact and Phrase we have already covered. Broad is like a more abstract Phrase and includes synonyms.

If someone searches water bottle in Amazon and there are three bidders on the keyword all bidding the same amount, Amazon will choose the Exact bidder above the Broad or Phrase. You can see from the screenshot that the Broad will need to pay 75c whereas the Exact only needs to pay 56c.

As automatic campaigns only use Broad, this can give the manual campaign quite a big advantage. Now enough of PPC, onto some cheaper ways of marketing your Amazon FBA products.

Amazon Search Optimisation

I am not an expert in keyword optimisation and what exactly it is that Amazon looks for when choosing the top organic results. But I can guess:

Your listing needs to be obviously a result related to the search term

Have good reviews

Have a high bestseller rank

Have good conversion rate

We will cover reviews and conversion in a later part of this article. Having a bestseller ranking is all about selling a lot within the last 24 hours (one of the reasons why it is worth doing PPC even if you just break even).

So that leaves us with being relevant for your search term. This is called keyword optimisation. The concept is simple:

You want to have the phrases and keywords that people are searching for appear in you listing

When you create your listing there are a few places where you can put keywords. I have numbered them in decreasing importance.

The name. – This is the title that appears at the top in bold.

The key features. – These are bullet points that appear at the top of the listing page.

The description. – This is a human-readable description further down the listing page.

The search terms section. – This is a back end section that customers can't read. It is only for Amazon.

You want to include your main keywords in the title. And then put your more unusual ones further down. And the really abstract ones that you can't get into your description place in the search terms.

Be a bit careful with the title. You want to balance telling Amazon exactly what the listing is about with keeping it attractive and readable for human beings. I am sure we've all seen keyword stacked Amazon listings that are unreadable. If your title is putting off human buyers, then you are doing something wrong.

As I said, I'm not an expert so I will avoid trying to give advice on keyword density or anything like that. Have a play around and see what works. If you're struggling to think of keywords, you can use those that convert well in the search terms report of your PPC advertising.

It is worth checking to make sure that Amazon is indexing your keywords. You can do this manually by searching for the keywords and seeing if your item appears. Or you can use a third party tool such as Keywordinspector. If your keyword isn't indexed you can contact seller support to try and get it added.

You can take this keyword optimization to a huge geek out level, and there are some pretty advanced tools out there to help you do it. Splity is the main one. It allows you to do split testing with your product pages. Basically, it will automatically try out different descriptions/titles/search terms and find the ones that convert the best.

They're very good but expensive. To track 500 keywords costs $97 a month, 100 costs $47 a month. It's pretty advanced so I don't recommend investing until you already have some sales and want to optimize further. A slight description change isn't going to take you from no sales to lots of sales. But it could take you from 50 sales a day to 60, which would more than cover the cost.

GETTING VIEWS ON YOUR LISTING FROM OUTSIDE AMAZON

The biggest difficulty when marketing your Amazon FBA business by getting more views from Amazon is that every other FBA seller is trying to do the exact same thing. It is very competitive and even if you're in a narrow specific niche, chances are there are at least a couple of other people trying to compete with you.

One solution is to move away from Amazon and try and get customers coming straight from an outside website to you listing.

Influencer Marketing – Getting Influential People To Recommend Your Item

The technique I have had the best results with is to contact websites that are recommending my competitors and asking them to consider my product.

Let me show you an example. Let's say I have just created a new yoga mat. My first step is to find out what review websites are appearing high on Google for relevant keywords. Stuff like:

What yoga mat should I buy

best yoga mat

top yoga mat on Amazon

You get the idea. Here is the fist page of Google for 'best yoga mat':

I have drawn a red box around every website that is making money from affiliate links to Amazon. That means that if you read one of their reviews, click through to Amazon and buy a yoga mat, they will earn a commission. If you're interested in learning more about affiliate links, that is how this blog makes money.Read my income report for a breakdown.

My tactic is to email every website and offer to send them one of my products to review. Some will agree to that, some will ignore the email, and some will ask to be paid. Whether it is worth paying for the review really depends and you'll need to use your own judgment to decide.

Websites aren't the only influencers who are worth targeting. Popular Instagram and YouTubers are also worth considering. They are both emerging markets and there are many content creators who don't know their worth. As such you can often find a popular Instagrammer in a niche who is willing to promote your product in exchange for just a free item.

I am sure there are a lot of other influencers out there you can target. Use your imagination! If you can find people who your competitors aren't approaching, that gives you a big advantage.

Giveaways & Deals On Offer Sites

People love a deal. And by offering your product at a ridiculously low price it can be quite easy to get a lot of sales. You aren't going to make any money from these sales, but you will help you climb the bestseller rankings and you will get some reviews out of it.

IMPORTANT NOTE: You cannot offer someone a discount in return for a review. But reviews that come as a side effect from offering a discount are fine. There are lots of websites and communities that allow you to list or promote discounted items from Amazon. One that was built specifically for Amazon is JumpSend.

You create a coupon code on Amazon and create a deal listing on JumpSend. Then whenever someone clicks through on your deal they will be given the coupon code to buy your product. It's also a pretty good site for finding very cheap deals on private label items.

Amazon's own Lightning Deals is another example. For a one off fee ($150 in use, £25 in UK) you can get Amazon to advertise your item on its deals page. You need to offer a large discount, it is only for a short time and you can limit the amount of stock available. To create a lightning deal go to 'Advertising -> Lightning Deals' in Seller Central.

JumpSend and Lightning Deals' biggest strength is also their biggest weakness. They are designed and optimised for Amazon. Which means that there is a good chance your competitors will also be using them. If you want a real competitive advantage, I suggest finding niche specific and non-Amazon related deal sites as well.

Pay-Per-Click Advertising
We've spoken a bit about pay-per-click advertising inside of Amazon. But it is worth being aware that there are lots of platforms outside of Amazon that also accept PPC advertising.

Here are a few places you might want to look into:

- Facebook Ads
- Reddit Ads
- Google Adwords
- Outbrain

Advertising on Instagram

It is very easy to sink a huge amount of money into advertising, so be careful. Start small and track how much you're spending vs how many extra sales you get. Only once you have a positive return on investment should you think about scaling up.

I won't go into this sort of advertising in a lot of detail here because I have previously written about it. Check out this post about how I use Outbrain to drive traffic to favorable reviews of my products, which then converts to more sales on Amazon.

IMPROVING THE CONVERSIONS OF YOUR LISTINGS

Marketing your Amazon FBA products isn't just about getting as many people as possible to view your listing. Once you have people viewing it, you want as many as possible to go on and purchase the product. This is known as conversion and is important for two reasons.

Improving conversions is a good way to make extra money without having to get more views on your listing.

A good conversion is a factor in determining how high you appear on Amazon searches and how much you pay for PPC advertising on Amazon.

Having A Top Quality Listing

The better your listing is the more likely someone is to buy your product. There are really two things you can optimize here:

Good Photographs (and videos!)

Your main photo needs to have a white background but apart from that Amazon doesn't seem to mind if you get a bit creative with your other photos. You can even include a video.

I suggest including anything you can to help convince a customer to buy your product: Answering common questions in the images. Such as a picture showing the dimension and weight.

Include text showing the products key features.

Show any awards your product has received.

Include anything that sets you apart. Such as a long warranty.

Make the products look awesome in the photo.

Taking good product photos is both an art and a science. You can try and take pictures yourself but the reality is that you probably won't be able to make them good enough. Which is a problem, because the cost to hire a top professional can run to many thousands.

We take a slightly more creative approach in my business. We search on Instagram for people who are in our niche and have made it a hobby to take amazing photographs of similar items. We contact them and pay them to photograph our products. So far this has been working well and is a lot cheaper than going to a dedicated product photographer.

Here are some good listings I've plucked from Amazon:

Just like every part of marketing your Amazon FBA business, there is no right or wrong way to do the product images. If it works and leads to extra sales then go for it. If you think of something creative that no one is doing, don't be afraid to give it a go! If you have lots of different images and not sure which ones are best, you can use Splity to test them and find the combination with the highest conversion.

Good Description

If you have a basic listing there isn't actually much freedom in what we can include on the product page. We are limited to just selecting a bunch of bullet points that appear below the title and a long form description that appears quite far down the page.

A lot of people won't read the description, but almost everyone will read the bullet point features. So make sure they are as good and convincing as possible. If you are selling on a marketplace that isn't in your native language, please please please get a native speaker to edit it for you.

Getting Good Reviews

People spend a lot of time worrying about getting as many reviews as possible. They are important but I have found that once you get above about 20 reviews there are real diminishing returns – each extra review only has a small impact on the customers' decision to buy your product. And having good reviews alone won't make you appear higher on Amazon searches. More important is to make sure that your reviews stay at an average of 4.5 stars or higher.

There are a lot of shady methods for getting reviews that I do not recommend. The advantages from getting a few extra reviews are outweighed by the risks of having your seller account closed because you broke some terms and conditions.

The one grey-area method I do recommend is to get your friends to buy your product and leave a review. Don't give them a discount and don't refund their purchase because that could be seen as review manipulation and get you in trouble with Amazon (and their reviews removed). After the initial few reviews, I like to set up automated emails asking customers to leave a review.

Amazon allows this but doesn't make it easy, there is no way to set up automated mass emails from inside Amazon Seller Central. Instead, we have to use a third party service.

I personally use Feedback Genius. It is very simple to use and has a lot of customizability. There are different plans to choose from but the smallest one is free and allows up to 100 emails a month. Then $20 for the next 1,000 emails.

There are a lot of rules about how you can use emails in marketing your Amazon FBA products. You cannot:

Incentivise a customer to leave a good review. That means no "get 20% off your next order if you leave a good review".

You cannot include a decision tree to filter different types of reviews. That means you are not allowed to say "if you loved the product click here to leave a good review, or if you were in any way unsatisfied please click here to message me directly and I will do everything I can to fix it".

You are also not allowed to include a link to your own website in the email.

If Amazon catches you breaking these rules you could lose your seller account.

So if you can't include any of that, what can you include to encourage them to leave a good review? My personal preference is a two email chain.

The first email simply includes useful information about their purchase and asks that if they are unhappy to email me. Here is my template for some table tennis bats I sell:

Hi [[first-name]],

My name is Sam and I'm one of the creators of the xxxx. Thank you so much for your order!

I wanted to reassure you that we've got you covered. If you aren't completely satisfied with something when your order arrives, then let me know and we'll get it straightened out for you ASAP.

Additionally, if you have any questions about your order or our products we'd be happy to help you out.

If you'd like to get in touch, you can just reply to this message and we'll respond promptly. No question is ever too small or unimportant.

I'm going to provide some usage tips for your xxxx:

After receiving your bat, the first step is to remove the protective film on each of the black and red rubbers. The rubbers should feel a bit sticky to the touch. It's this surface that enables you to create the incredible spin that our bats are known for.

The bat should be stored in its case between use. If left out for a prolonged period of time the rubbers should be cleaned. As you use the bat, the rubbers will start to attract dust from the ball and will lose their feeling of stickiness. They can be cleaned by wiping them down with a bit of water on a clean cloth.

After about a year of heavy usage, the rubbers will slowly lose their spin and should be replaced. They are designed to be easily removed and new rubbers can be stuck down in their place. Alternatively, a new bat can be purchased.

The bat has been tested and approved by the International Table Tennis Federation, meaning its legal for use at tournaments of any level. So go, win some matches and enjoy the bat!

All the best,

Sam

This email sets the tone for the level of customer service I want to offer as well as heading off bad reviews before they happen. If someone complains and I can't fix their issue, I just don't send them the next email.

Remember, good customer service is another way of marketing your Amazon FBA business. If people have a good experience they will tell other people leading to more sales.

My second email asks for a review:

Hey [[first-name]],

First off, I wanted to say thank you once again for your support. Our small business wouldn't be able to grow and continue to produce top quality table tennis bats without your help.

I noticed your order was delivered a couple days ago, so I hope that you've had the chance to try it out and make sure you are happy with everything.

We are always aiming to improve our products and service, and we would really appreciate if you could take 2 seconds to provide us with some feedback:

[[product-review-link:Leave a review]]Thank you again for your trust and support.

As always, if you have any questions, suggestions or comments, or even just want to have a chat, send us a message by replying to this email and we'll get back to you as soon as possible.

All the best,

Sam

The text in square brackets is shortcode which Feedback Genius converts into links that are customised for each customer.

Once again experiment with the wording of your emails. Ohh and if you find any good tricks please drop me an email to let me know.

GET MARKETING YOUR AMAZON FBA BUSINESS

To wrap up, I really want top reiterate what I said at the beginning. Marketing only works when everyone isn't doing it. If you can think of ideas for marketing your Amazon FBA products that aren't on this list, then give it a go and if it works stick with it. Don't follow the crowd. Use your own creativity. And don't be afraid to try and fail different ideas.

PROS & CONS OF THE THREE TYPES OF AMAZON FBA BUSINESS

There are three types of Amazon FBA business, what I am calling 'Retail Arbitrage', 'Private Labelling' and 'Brand Building', and everyone gets confused between the three. So let me break them down for you. They each have pros and cons and if you're going to start an Amazon FBA business you need to choose one.

Retail Arbitrage

Retail Arbitrage is very simple. You find products that are cheap in the real world (or online) and sell them for a profit on Amazon.

A mythical day in the life of a retail arbitrager:

You get up early because you have a long day of hunting products ahead. First stop, a car boot sale where you scan all the second-hand books trying to find gems. You are there a couple of hours and return home with a car full of books.

Next stop is your local supermarket to see what they have on discount. You find a certain toy is a half price and your app tells you it is selling well on Amazon. You buy every single one in the shop, and then you spend the next six hours driving round to all the other branches in a 100 miles radius and buying all their stock too.

Once home you start packing and uploading all your goodies to Amazon. You print off the pre-paid labels from UPS, book in a collection and go to bed. On the collection date Amazon picks up your parcels and a few days later they are on sale on Amazon.

Pros:

1. You need very little money to start.
2. You know how well the items are selling before you buy them.

3. You learn the ropes of Amazon and Amazon FBA. And you can use the knowledge (and money earned) to have a higher chance of success with the other two business models.
4. It is very easy. There are apps that let you scan an item's barcode and will tell you if you can sell it for a profit on Amazon (and how much you'll make after fees). Profit Bandit is the most popular.

Cons:

You aren't building a business. You will make money provided you put the time it, but as soon as you stop the business ceases to exist. That means that your business has very little value and will be difficult to sell.

You can make a lot of money from it (6/7 figures), but it takes a lot of practice and dedication to get that good. Most people make far far less.

You are reliant on Amazon's good will. If you make a mistake by selling a product you're not allowed to you could risk losing the account and business.

Final Thoughts

Retail Arbitrage is a real hustle where the hardest workers do the best. When compared to the other two it doesn't look very attractive: you aren't building a sellable business, the amount you earn is linked to how hard you work (like a job) and the more people who start doing it the harder your job will be. But, and it's a big but. You don't need much money to start, and that's a really big advantage. Realistically I wouldn't recommend trying either of the other two methods without at least £5,000 to invest. Yes, you can do it for less, but it is very difficult. Whereas retail arbitrage can be started with £100.

A lot of people treat retail arbitrage as a cheap 'Amazon FBA University'. You get hands on experience with Amazon works and how to tell what sells, all without ever having to risk much money. Then once you have built up some decent profits and are an expert on the inner workings of Amazon you can start a private label business or a brand.

Private Labelling

Private labelling is a bit more complicated. You find a gap in the market for a product and you get the product made cheaply under your own private brand. You don't care what the product is as long as there is demand and little competition.

A mythical day in the life of a private labeller:

You get up whenever you like and check your previous night's sales. You have earned money in your sleep! But you also have 10 customer service messages to respond to. You then check your current inventory levels and reorder what you are low on. One of your products is not selling and looks like it needs to be liquidated. You contact a liquidator to take it off your hands.

You then spend the next few hours searching for new niches. You are using a product like Jungle Scout to search the Amazon backend and find products that are selling well with bad reviews, indicating an unfilled demand. After a few hours you start to feel cross-eyed from too long staring at numbers so stop, but you have a few potential items: a pillow, some tupperware and a toy cactus.

Next you head over to Alibaba to find some factories who can produce the items for you. You spend the next few hours contacting factories and asking for samples. You then spend the final hour before bed paying all your outstanding bills. You owe tax, factories and freight forwarders. All in different currencies.

Pros

1. This is probably where people are making the most money on Amazon. The top few are earning 7 or 8 figures a year.
2. Each product you add compounds your earnings. Meaning that your monthly profit goes up every month.
3. Your risk is spread across a lot of different unrelated products. One failure doesn't affect your business.

Cons

1. You are totally reliant on Amazon. If they go bankrupt or the site closes then your business disappears.
2. You have a high chance of purchasing a bad/unprofitable product on your first few attempts. If you haven't budgeted for that, your business could be over before you even begin.
3. You are very susceptible to competition. If another private labeller spots the same gap in the market as you then you end up competing.
4. It is cash intensive. You are always purchasing new stock and prototypes.
5. You have to manage a very large catalogue of different products. It is time intensive.

6. You spend half your life dealing with Chinese/Indian factories.

Final Thoughts

Private labelling has somewhat of a bad reputation and many 'serious businessmen' see it as a get rich quick scheme. This isn't helped by the hundreds of 'gurus' and extortionately priced courses out there promising to teach you how to do it. Some of which are good, but most of which aren't far off a scam. But what no one can argue with are the results that the top private labellers are achieving. Amazon FBA private labelling has made a lot of millionaires.

But do not mistake the huge potential earnings for easy money. To be the best takes a lot of work and a lot of experience, you will not stumble across one niche that will make you a fortune. The trick is in continually adding products and non-stop research. For every private label millionaire, there are 1,000 people making £1,000 a month. And for every person making £1,000 a month, there is someone who chose the wrong product and lost their money.

I think of private labellers as modern day merchants. They spend their time hunting out opportunities where there are good cheap items for sale in one country, and not in another. Then they stick their brand on top to stop others from piggybacking on their hard-work.

Brand Building

Building a brand is by far my favourite type of Amazon FBA business. You pick a niche you are familiar with and then build different products under your brand name around that niche. You have a much smaller range than a private labeller, but your margins are much higher and they are all focused on your one niche and often lead to cross-sales between products.

A mythical day in the life of a brand owner:

You wake up whenever you feel like it and check your previous night's sales. You have earned money in your sleep! Because you only have a few different products your inventory projections are done well in advance leaving your supply chain takes care of itself.

You then spend the next few hours contacting influencers in your niche. You scour Instagram, messaging everyone in your niche with over 1,000 followers. Asking if they want a free item and a commission on any sales they generate. You then start writing an article for your brand's blog. An analysis of the latest event/gossip in your niche. Once done you post a link to it on every forum you can find.

It's now thinking time. You grab a glass of wine and sit in your arm chair, thinking up ideas for innovative products or for new marketing stunts. You have an idea and send it to your factory/designer to get a prototype knocked up.

In the evening you jump in the car and go a social event for people in your niche. You're not there to sell, just to make friends and remind them your product exists.

Pros

- You aren't as susceptible to competition. People are buying your product because of the brand, not because it is cheap. Your margins are also higher.
- Your brand is independent of Amazon. So if Amazon goes bankrupt or closes your seller account, then you can move your brand and sell elsewhere. Any work gone into building the brand is still there.
- You will know your niche well before you start and will be able to easily contact and sell to initial customers.
- Your brand has value and therefore means it is worth more than a private label company making the same profit.

Cons

- Building a brand's reputation takes a long time, like years. It is a commitment.
- If you choose the wrong niche it is hard to move.
- Bad reviews (especially early on) are really damaging. You need to be careful to be liked by the people in your niche.
- You need to make sure your products are really good. That means a lot more prototyping and back and forth with factories.

Final Thoughts

I've already said that brand building is my favourite type of Amazon FBA business and you've probably guessed that it is the one I focus on myself. Brand building has existed forever, but whereas once-upon-a-time you would need to invest in a storefront, a warehouse, a distribution network and customer service representatives – now Amazon FBA handles it all for you. That means that instead of needing £200,000 to start a brand, you can do it with just a fraction of the amount.

I often get asked is Amazon FBA is saturated. Well there are a lot of people using Amazon FBA, but the question doesn't really make sense when talking about starting a brand. It doesn't matter how many people start private labelling or retail arbitraging as long as there is demand in your niche, on or off Amazon.

EVERY TOOL I USE FOR MY AMAZON SELLER BUSINESS

Market Research

I recently wrote a whole article about market research for Amazon FBA. In it, I completed raved about my favourite Amazon seller tool: Jungle Scout. It's seriously awesome and powerful. And the more I use it the more I like it. Jungle Scout lets you very easily dive into Amazon and getting all sort of useful information about your potential competitors and choose where you'll position your niche. It even includes approximate monthly sales.

The Chrome extension costs $87 one-off and works with the UK and USA marketplaces. Or the Web App (which I use) is $69 a month for the version that includes the Niche Hunter (my favourite tool) or £39 for just the product database. It only works with the USA marketplace.

EDIT: The Web App now works for all marketplaces and not just the USA.

If I'd known about Jungle Scout when I first started it would have saved me from a lot of the rookie Amazon seller mistakes I made.

Sourcing Your Product

I find all my suppliers on Alibaba. The basic website and a lot of the stuff sold on it are pretty awful. But it does give you a very easy way to find and get in touch with a lot of factories in countries where it is very cheap to produce products. It's free to contact the suppliers. But they will often charge you to send you samples.

I've been able to run a profitable Amazon seller business involving multiple factories building my own unique products. All without ever leaving my bedroom. I have never been to China. I have never even spoken to anyone on the phone. I communicate completely through email or sometimes skype messages. All thanks to Alibaba and the contacts I made through it.

Cheap Foreign Currency Payments

If you do a normal bank transfer or Paypal payment for a large amount of foreign currency you will get burnt with huge exchange fees. To get round them I use CurrencyFair. It's a marketplace where your currency is exchanged with another user for free. Similar to how the stock market works. You don't pay any conversion fees, but there is a small fee for any withdrawals. Currently, it is £2.5.

I normally get the same exchange rate that is being quoted on Google. So the only cost is the withdrawal fee. On a £10,000 transfer, a £2.5 fee is nothing. It would cost closer to £300 to do a regular bank transfer. The only issue with CurrencyFair is that the payments aren't instant. But for a £300 saving, I think it is well worth it.

Import, Logistics and Customs Clearance

I use Flexport for all my logistics and dealing with customs. All that stuff is a minefield and as I am sending inventory to multiple countries with lots of different laws, it makes sense to outsource it all. Flexport is a Google-backed venture that aims to bring logistics into the web era.

Unfortunately, they are currently only accepting new clients who are doing over 5,000kg of freight a year. So if you are a smaller seller, here are some options you could try instead:

Shapiro – I've never used them but they recommended by Amazon.

Fedex or DHL– Very easy to use and you can send straight from your supplier to the Amazon FBA warehouses. It is probably the cheapest option for shipments under 100kg.

Warehousing & Fulfilment

I use Amazon FBA for single item fulfilment. Unfortunately, you need to pay Amazon per item in the order. Even if you're selling hundreds to a single buyer. To get round that huge cost I use Shipwire for any wholesale fulfilment. Provided I'm selling full cartons it works out very cheap.

That being said, I have had some bad experiences with Shipwire. They can be slow and they only work in dollars. Ok, I know they're not an Amazon seller tool. But if you are building a brand then wholesaling to physical retailers should definitely be in your long-term plan.

Marketing

I have three marketing streams:

- Amazon PPC adverts.
- Marketing through a well-read blog.
- Through organic traffic from Amazon.

Getting Reviews

I have found that the number and quality of reviews on your product on Amazon are hugely important for getting sales. But most people don't leave a review, so if you leave it to build organically it could take hundreds of sales before even getting one. Which means potentially thousands of missed sales before your product looks trustable.

One tactic for getting more reviews that I like to do is to email each customer personally. Unfortunately, Amazon doesn't let you send out automated emails and if I had to do it manually I'd be typing all day. Luckily there is a third party website known as Feedback Genius that does it for you.

On Feedback Genius, you can set up automated emails that contain. It also ties in with all marketplaces, so I can send my personal friendly emails in different languages depending on what Amazon they purchased from.

My email strategy is pretty simple. I try and sound personal and like we are a small brand (which we are). Then I try and set them up to only leave good reviews: "If you didn't like the product then email me, otherwise please leave a good review".

Feedback Genius is only $20 a month for up to 1,000 emails a month. To me, that's a real no-brainer.

Bookkeeping And Accountancy

I use Xero UK (click here for the USA version) for all my accounting and bookkeeping. It's not specifically for Amazon sellers, in fact I use it for every one of my businesses, but it does work great with Amazon.

You link up your Amazon seller and bank accounts to it, and Xero reconciles everything and provides you with every report imaginable. I also use it to file my VAT and other tax returns.

Xero currently costs either £22 or £27.5 a month depending on whether you need multi-currency. I do because I sell in USD, CAD and EUR as well as £.

I use a plugin called A2X to automate the linking of my Amazon seller centrals to Xero. A2X is currently $59 a month for each continent (and there's a 10% forever discount with code TRYA2X19_10%OFF). I therefore need two subscriptions to cover both the Americas and Europe.

A2X isn't a necessity. You can do it manually if you want, and you probably should if you're not making much money. But it's quite a lot of manual work copying and pasting the information from two invoices a month from each marketplace into Xero, and it's very easy to make mistakes.

Fulfillment by Amazon (FBA) is an e-commerce service in which third-party vendors store their products in Amazon's fulfillment centers and the e-commerce giant picks, sorts, packs, ships, tracks and handles returns and refunds for these products. In addition to accounting for a huge portion of Amazon's revenue, FBA enables Amazon to offer other vendors' products alongside its own.

FBA gives smaller vendors access to Amazon's web-to-warehouse picking and sorting system and other logistics services, freeing the vendor to focus more on other aspects of their business. Amazon charges merchants for storage space and a fee for orders it fulfills. Shipping costs and 24/7 customer service are included in vendor fees.

HOW FULFILLMENT BY AMAZON (FBA) WORKS

To sign up for FBA, merchants in the United States, Canada and Mexico need a Selling on Amazonaccount. Merchants can add products to the Amazon catalog one at a time, in bulk or by integrating their inventory management software with Amazon, using Amazon's application program interface (API). Listings on the Amazon website are shown with the Amazon Prime logo. There is no additional charge for Amazon Prime free two-day shipping, and there is free shipping on eligible orders. FBA can also be integrated into vendors' websites so that customers can do their shopping through Amazon without leaving the third-party's website.

Amazon advises merchants that use its e-commerce service to ensure their products are "e-commerce-ready" so they can be safely and securely transported to customers. Amazon makes polybags, boxes, stretch wrap, bubble pack and other shipping materials easily available to Selling on Amazon vendors. Some fees for Selling on Amazon and optional services may be applicable

SELLING YOUR PRODUCTS ON AMAZON: A BRAND'S GUIDE
Join HuffPost Plus

As Amazon has soared to dominate ecommerce, many retail brands have started to inquire about how they can take advantage of the platform's features to increase their brand awareness and online sales. There's no doubt about it, Amazon is a force to be reckoned with, but if brands aren't informed, prepared to handle the demand, and maintaining close attention their selling strategy, things can spin out of control.

As a brand, if you're interested in selling on Amazon, here are few things to consider before you push your product listings live:

STOCK UP

Ensure that you have enough product inventory available to ship your Amazon orders, and closely monitor your stock levels as your products begin to sell. As a seller, if you have a product listed that is not in stock, Amazon will penalize your account.

Your products need to be shipped out in a timely manner, and within the timeframe you state on your product listing page. If you'd prefer not to handle fulfillment yourself, to save time or streamline your operations, Amazon does Fulfillment by Amazon (FBA) for a fee. Evaluate this offering against your business needs and budget to determine if FBA is right for you.

REVIEWS RULE

An astounding 84% of consumers trust online reviews as much as personal recommendations. Having reviews for your products adds credibility and helps prospective customers feel more informed about their purchasing decision. A great way to continue to build up your review count is to ask your customers post-purchase for a review.

While the more reviews your product listing has, the better, in an ideal world it's best to have an average rating of 4 to 5 stars. Be aware that negative reviews will easily tarnish your brand reputation and affect your selling performance. If you do receive negative reviews, time is of the essence. Respond quickly to any negative reviews you receive so you can demonstrate your brand's commitment to high quality customer service and your products, and make things right with your unhappy customer. Any customer questions should also be handled in a similar fashion, quickly and helpfully, to inch towards that conversion.

CONTENT IS KING

As you begin to build out your product listing pages, be sure to include detailed product information and any attributes that will increase your product's search visibility. Any keywords that a consumer would type into that search bar to find your product should be integrated into your listing page. Other details such as product dimensions and weight further inform your customer.

The photos you include for your listing should be high quality professional imagery to showcase your product. Consumers are also starting to expect video content, and enjoy the dynamic experience of seeing a product in action. Including a video on your product listing page further enhances the Amazon shopping experience.

THE BUY BOX

The holy grail of Amazon for sellers is getting control of that buy box. Amazon determines which seller to feature based on a proprietary algorithm which evaluates the seller's price, the fulfillment options available, and the seller rating. Getting featured on the buy box is extremely competitive. In an ideal world, if a seller has a 99% rating, uses FBA, and beats the next lowest price by 2-3%, then they will be featured in the buy box almost 100% of the time. It's important to focus on your pricing to ensure yours is the lowest available, and as the owner of the brand, your pricing should be.

WHAT PRICE IS RIGHT

Amazon shoppers are extremely price sensitive and are searching for the lowest price for the product they want. As a seller, changing your pricing on a whim and below what you can afford to sell at to get the lowest price listed will impact your bottom line as well as cause a chain reaction with 3rd party sellers. You also need to be aware of the prices 3rd party sellers are listing for your products. If their prices are lower than what you, as the brand, can afford to sell your own product at your established minimum retail price, something's up.

As a brand, it's imperative to gain control of your pricing by going after 3rd party sellers, to ensure they are not selling below the minimum advertised price per your brand's pricing guidelines. Sell inventory only to companies that sign contracts with you to adhere to pricing guidelines. You also need to prohibit resale besides your pre-approved retail outlets. For 3rd-party sellers that are not complying with your established retail pricing, figure out where they are getting inventory from, and tell them to stop. This requires time and effort to play detective, and you may need to get help from your brand's legal team to help you pursue these vendors. Amazon will not remove 3rd-party sellers or reinforce a price for all sellers. It's up to sellers to do this.

ADVERTISING OPTIONS

Amazon's in-house media group (AMG) and marketing services (AMS) pride themselves on their ability to seamlessly integrate advertising throughout the platform in a way that does not seem intrusive or disrupt consumers' shopping experience. With ad placement options in search results, headline search, and product display, as well as the ability to target customers on Amazon that exhibit similar behavior as your typical brand website consumers, Amazon offers a powerful tool for you to leverage your user behavior data and increase your ROI.

Printed in Dunstable, United Kingdom